MY BIG WORDBOOK

1100

WORDS

MOONSTONE

Aa

Afraid

Alligator

Abacus

Afternoon

Almond

Accident

Air

Alphabet

Acorn

Air conditioner

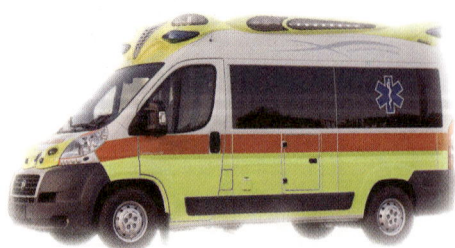

Ambulance

Aeroplane

Alarm clock

Anchor

2

Angry

Antelope

Apricot

Animal

Anthill

Aquarium

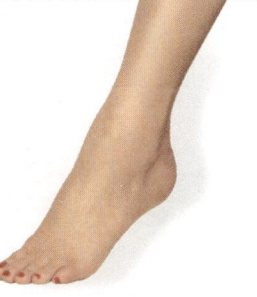

Ankle

Ape

Arc

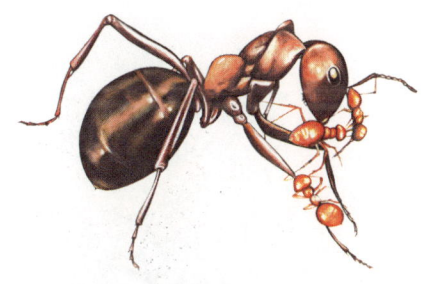

Ant

Aphid

Arch

Antbird

Apple

Arm

Armadillo

Asparagus

Avocado

Armchair

Astronaut

Awake

Armlet

Aunt

Arrow

Aurora

Award

Artist

Autumn

Axe

Bb

Bag

Bamboo

Baboon

Baker

Banana

Baby

Balcony

Bandage

Bacon

Ball

Barbeque

Badge

Balloon

Barber

Bark

Battery

Bear

Basket

Beach

Bed

Bat

Bead

Bed Sheet

Barrel

Beak

Bedroom

Bathroom

Bean

Bee

Beehive

Bench

Bison

Beetle

Bicycle

Black

Beetroot

Bird

Blanket

Bell

Birthday

Blender

Belt

Biscuit

Blind

Block

Body

Box

Blouse

Bone

Boy

Blue

Book

Branch

Blueberry

Bottle

Bread

Boat

Bowl

Breakfast

8

Brick

Brother

Bud

Bride

Brown

Buddy

Bridge

Brush

Buffalo

Broccoli

Bubble

Bugle

Broom

Bucket

Builder

9

Building

Bungalow

Bus stop

Bull

Burger

Butcher

Bulldozer

Butter

Bun

Burrow

Butterfly

Bunch

Bus

Button

10

C c

Calf

Candy

Cabbage

Camel

Cantaloupe

Cage

Camera

Cap

Cake

Camp

Car

Calendar

Candle

Caribou

Carpenter

Cartoon

Cauliflower

Carpet

Castle

Cave

Carriage

Cat

Celery

Carrot

Catch

Chain

Cart

Caterpillar

Chair

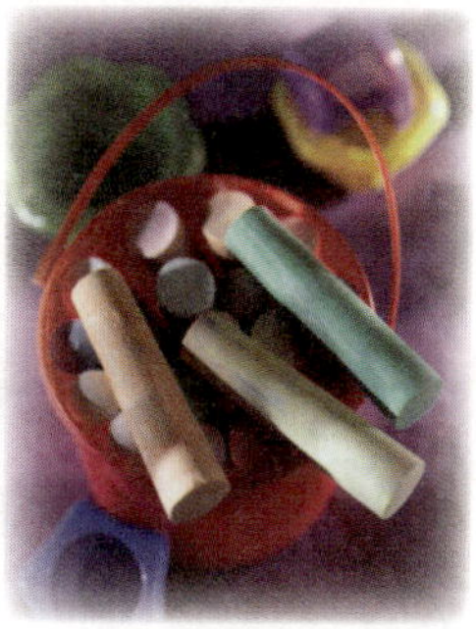

Chalk

Cheetah

Chilli

Chalkboard

Cherry

Chimney

Chart

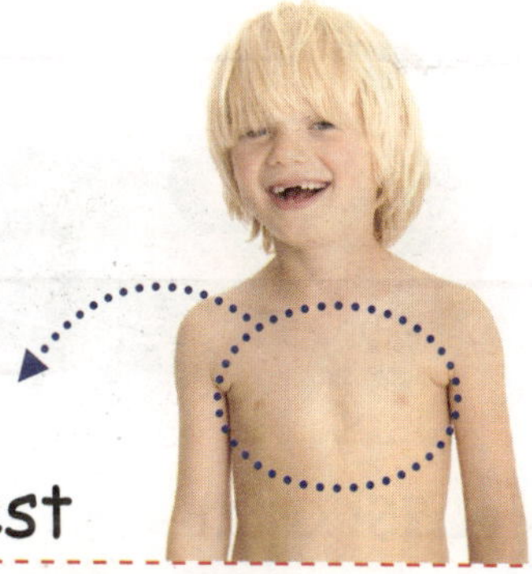

Chest

Chimpanzee

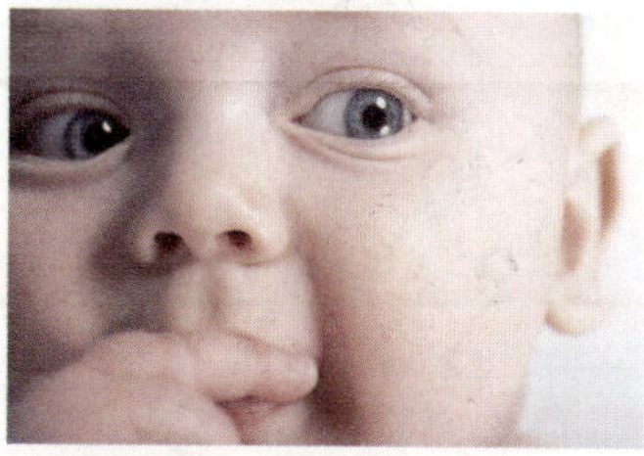

Cheek

Chick

Chin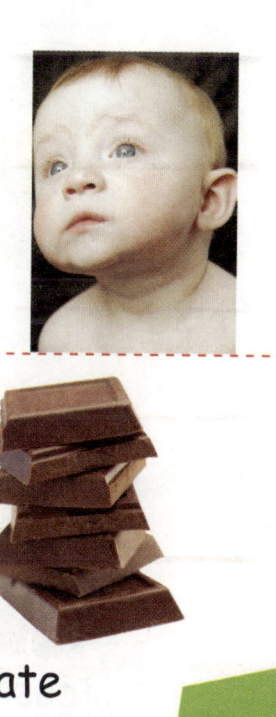

Cheese

Child

Chocolate

Chopstick

City

Clerk

Church

Clap

Climb

Cinema

Classroom

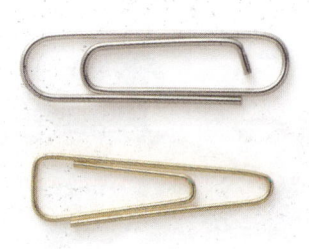

Clip

Circle

Clean

Clock

Circus

Clear

Cloth

Cloud

Cobra

Coffee

Clown

Cock

Coin

Coast

Cockatoo

Cold

Coat

Cockroach

College

Cobbler

Coconut

Colour

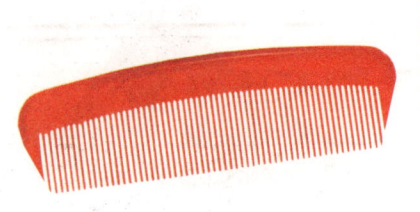

Comb

Corn

Cousin

Computer

Corner

Cow

Cone

Couch

Crab

Cook

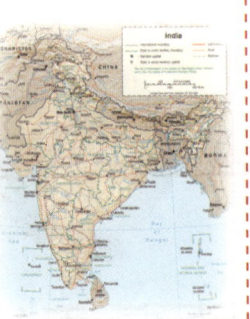

Count

Crane

Coral

Country

Crawl

Crayon

Crowd

Cupboard

Cricket

Crown

Curtain

Crocodile

Cry

Cushion

Crop

Cucumber

Custard apple

Crow

Cup

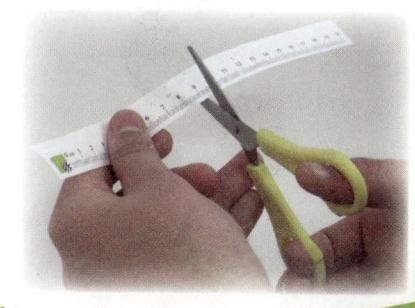
Cut

Dd

Daughter

Desk

Dance

Day

Dessert

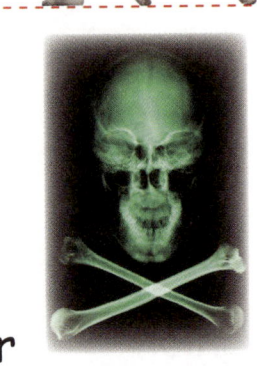
Danger

Decorate

Diamond

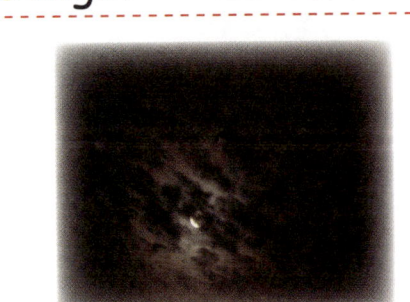
Dark

Deer

Dinner

Date

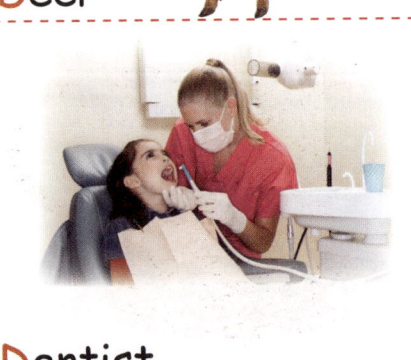
Dentist

Direction

Dirty

Dog

Doughnut

Dishwasher

Doll

Dragonfly

Dive

Dolphin

Divide

Donkey

Draw

Doctor

Door

Drawer

Dream

Drop

Dustbin

Dress

Drum

Duster

Dresser

Duck

Dustpan

Dressing gown

Duckling

Dwarf

Drink

Dust

Dynamite

Ee

Earthworm

Elbow

Eagle

Eat

Electricity

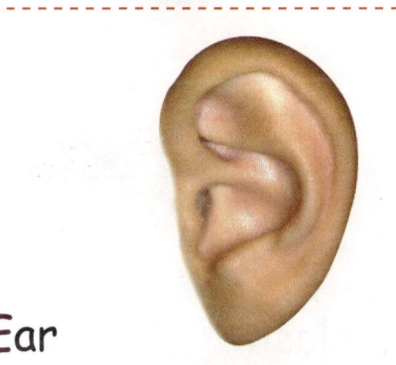

Ear

Egg

Elephant

Earth

Eggplant

Engine

Earthquake

Eight

Engineer

Envelope

Evening

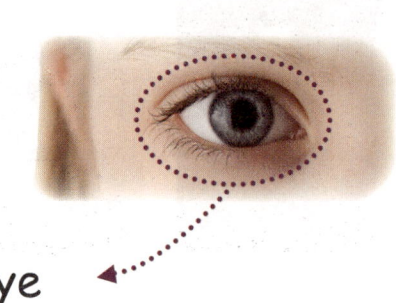

Eye

Eraser

Exercise

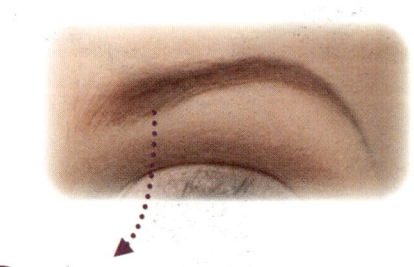

Eyebrow

Escalator

Eyelash

Eskimo

Explode

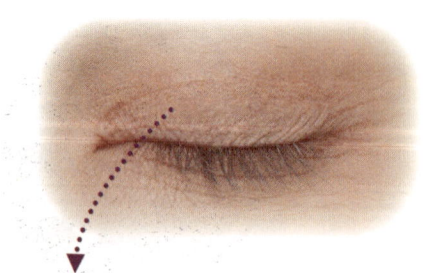

Eyelid

Essay

Eyeliner

Ff

Family

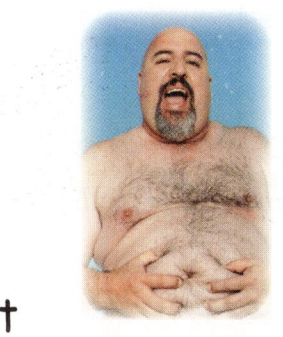
Fat

Face

Fan

Father

Factory

Farm

Faucet

Falcon

Farmer

Fear

Fall

Fast

Feather

Fence

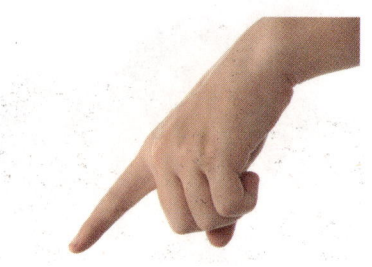

Finger

Firefly

Field

Finish

Fireman

Fight

Fire

Fireplace

Film

Fire engine

First aid

Find

Fire station

Fish

Fisherman

Flea

Flour

Fishing

Float

Flower

Flag

Flood

Flute

Flamingo

Floor

Fly

Flashlight

Florist

Foal

Fog

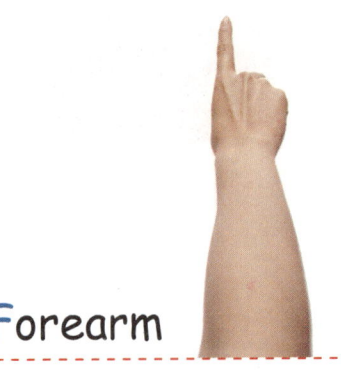

Forearm

Fox

Food

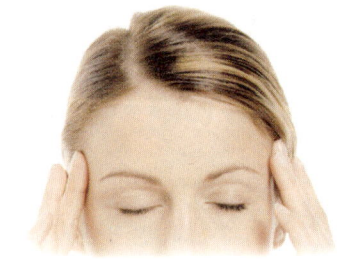

Forehead

Friend

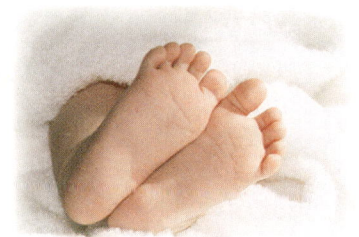

Foot

Forest

Frog

Football

Fork

Fruit

Force

Fountain

Furniture

Gg

Gate

Girl

Game

Ghost

Glass

Garbage

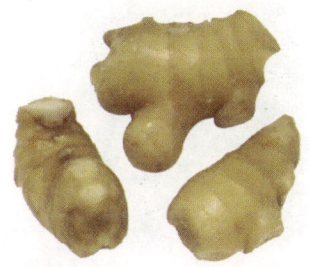
Gift

Glass

Garden

Ginger

Glide

Gardener

Giraffe

Globe

Glove

Goldfish

Grape

Glow

Goose

Grass

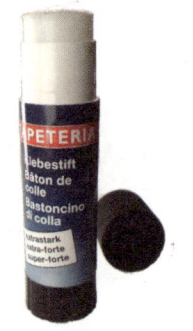
Glue

Gorilla

Grasshopper

Goat

Grandfather

Green

Gold

Grandmother

Grocery

Ground

Guardsman

Gumboot

Groundnut

Guava

Gun

Group

Guinea pig

Gym

Grove

Guitar

Gymnast

Grow

Gulf

Gypsy

Hh

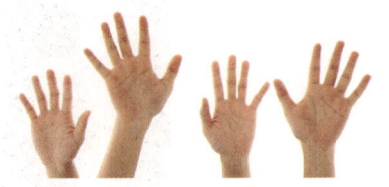

Hand

Harbour

Hair

Handkerchief

Harp

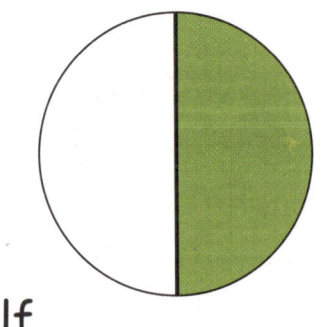

Hairbrush

Handle

Hat

Half

Hang

Hatch

Hammer

Happy

Hawk

30

Hay

Heat

High

Head

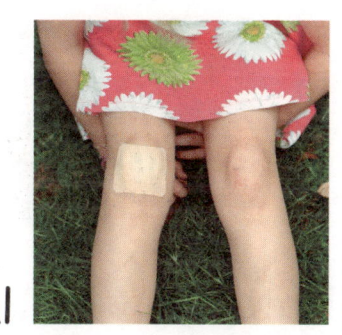
Heal

Hill

Headphone

Helicopter

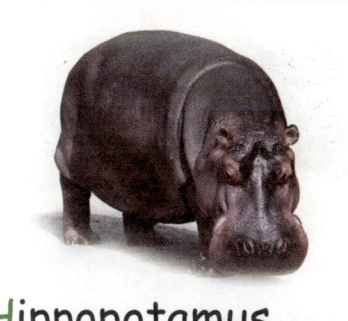
Hippopotamus

Hear

Helmet

Hockey

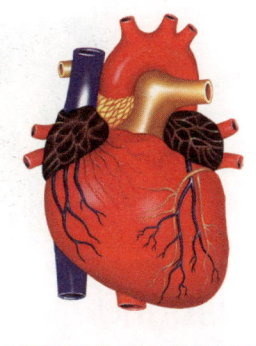
Heart

Hen

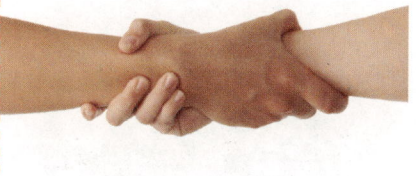
Hold

Holiday

Hotdog

Hummingbird

Honey

Hotel

Hungry

Honeycomb

House

Hurt

Horse

Housefly

Hut

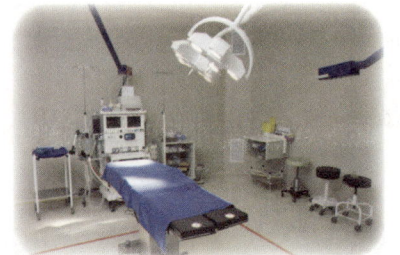
Hospital

Hug

Husband

Ice hockey

Iguana

Ibex

Iceberg

Ill

Ice

Iced tea

Impala

Ice bucket

Icicle

Indoor

Ice cream

Igloo

Infant

33

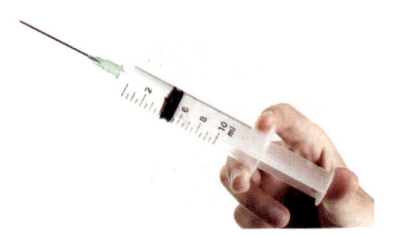

Injection

Inspect

Irrigation

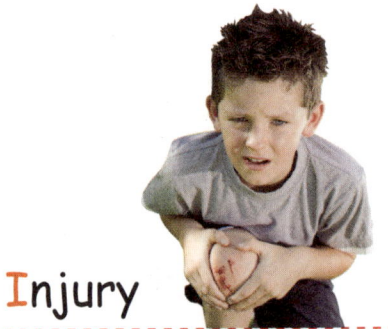

Injury

Internet

Island

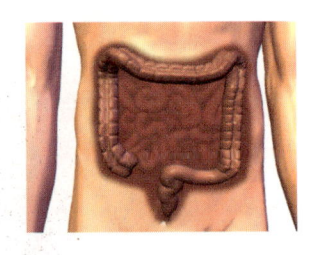

Ink

Intestine

Ivory

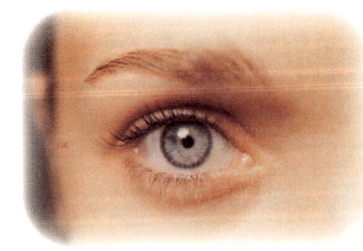

Inn

Iris

Insect

Iron

Ivy

Jj

Jar

Jeep

Jacket

Jasmine

Jelly

Jackfruit

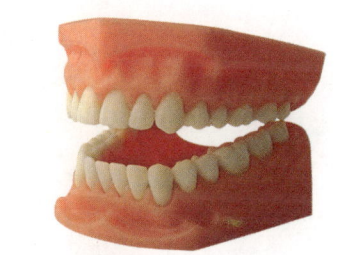
Jaw

Jellyfish

Jaguar

Jeans

Jet

Jewellery

Jigsaw

Judo

Jumpsuit

Jog

Jug

Jungle

Journey

Juice

Junglefowl

Joy

Jukebox

Junkyard

Judge

Jump

Jute

Kk

Key

Kid

Kangaroo

Keyboard

Kayak

Keyhole

King

Kennel

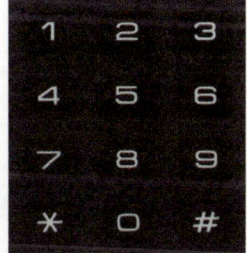

Keypad

Kingfisher

Kettle

Kick

Kiss

Kitchen	Knee	Koala
Kite	Knife	Kohlrabi
Kitten	Knob	Krill
Kiwi	Knock	Kulfi
Kiwi fruit	Knuckle	Kurta

L l

Ladybug

Lantern

Lace

Lake

Lap

Ladder

Lamb

Laugh

Ladle

Lamp

Lawn

Lady finger

Land

Lazy

39

Leader

Lemon

Lie

Leaf

Leopard

Lift

Leek

Letter

Light

Left

Lettuce

Lightening

Leg

Library

Lilac

Lily

Llama

Lollipop

Limb

Load

Lorry

Limousine

Lobster

Loud

Lion

Lock

Lunch

Lip

Log

Lychee

Mm

Mailbox

Market

Macaw

Man

Mask

Mango

Mat

Machine

Magazine

Map

Match

Maglev

Marble

Matchbox

Mattress

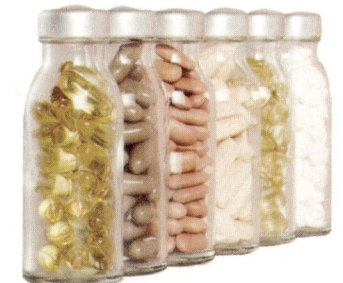
Medicine

Monkey

Meal

Melt

Monster

Measure

Milk

Moon

Meat

Mirror

Morning

Mechanic

Money

Mosque

Mosquito

Mouse

Muscle

Moth

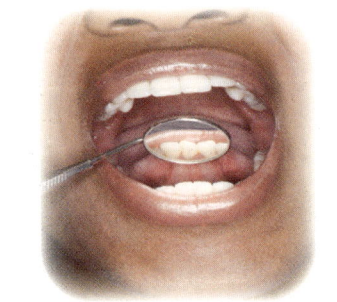
Mouth

Museum

Mother

Move

Mushroom

Motorcycle

Mud

Music

Mountain

Mug

Mussel

N n

Naughty

Needle

Nail

Navy

Neem

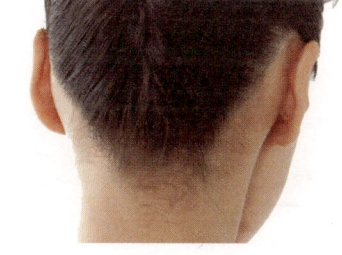
Nail clippers

Neck

Neighbour

Nail polish

Necklace

Nephew

Napkin

Necktie

Nest

Net

Noise

Nurse

Newspaper

Noodle

Nursery

Niece

Nose

Nut

Night

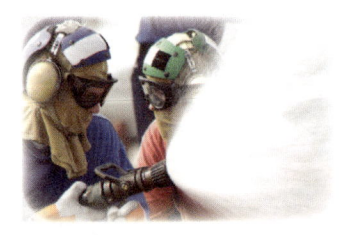
Nozzle

Nut shell

Nib

Number

Nylon

Oo

Octopus

Omelette

Oar

Office

Onion

Oasis

Oil

Opal

Oatmeal

Old

Open

Ocean

Olive

Opossum

Orange

Orchestra

Oval

Orangutan

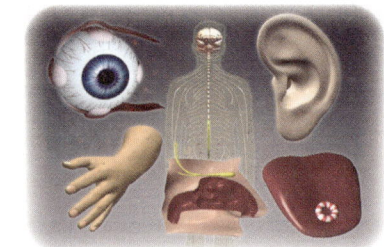
Organ

Oven

Orbit

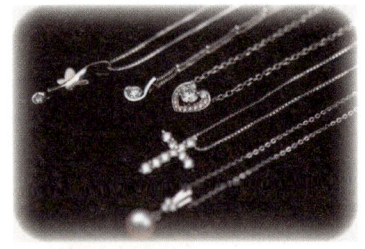
Ornament

Owl

Orchard

Oscar

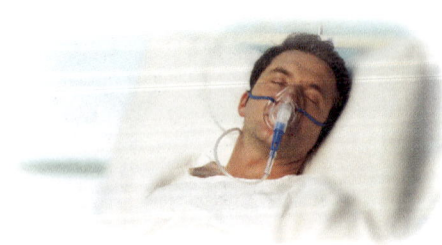
Oxygen

Orchid

Ostrich

Oyster

P p

Pair

Paper

Page

Palm

Parachute

Pain

Pan

Parcel

Paint

Panda

Park

Painter

Papaya

Parrot

Pavement

Peel

People

Pea

Pelican

Pepper

Peach

Pen

Pet

Peacock

Pencil

Petal

Pear

Penguin

Photograph

Photographer

Pillow

Pipe

Piano

Pilot

Pizza

Picnic

Pin

Plant

Pig

Pineapple

Plate

Pigeon

Pink

Play

Plumber

Polar bear

Ponytail

Pocket

Policeman

Pool

Poem

Pollen

Popsicle

Pomegranate

Port

Point

Pond

Postman

52

Pot

Prize

Puppet

Potato

Pull

Pup

Pour

Pumpkin

Purple

Prawn

Punch

Purse

Praying mantis

Pupil

Python

Qq

Quarter

Queue

Quack

Queen

Quiet

Quill

Quesadilla

Quail

What is your name?

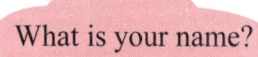

How are you?

Where do you live?

Question

Quilt

Quarrel

Quetzal

Quiz

Rr

Rain

Rattle

Rabbit

Rainbow

Read

Race

Raincoat

Ready

Radio

Raspberry

Rectangle

Radish

Rat

Red

55

Refrigerator

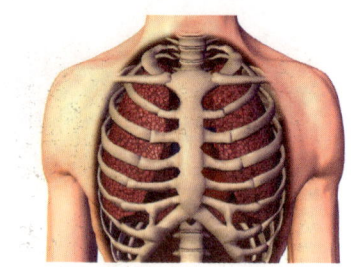
Ribcage

Road sign

Restaurant

Rice

Road roller

Rhinoceros

Ring

Roar

Rhombus

River

Robin

Ribbon

Road

Rock

Rocket

Rooster

Rubbish

Roller coaster

Root

Rubble

Rolling pin

Rope

Rudder

Roof

Rose

Ruler

Room

Rubber

Run

Ss

Salad

Saucer

Sack

Salt

Sausage

Sad

Sand

Scallop

Saddle

Sandal

Scarf

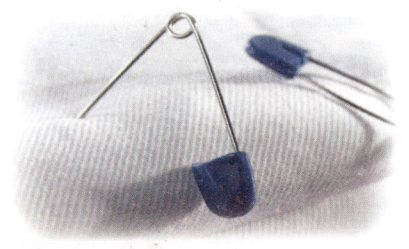
Safety pin

Sandwich

School

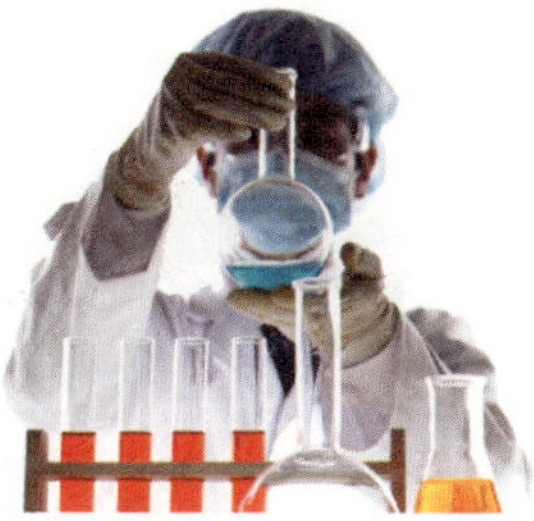

Scientist	Screwdriver	Shadow
Scissors	Sea	Shampoo
Scorpion	Seahorse	Shape
Scream	Seal	Shark
Screw	See-saw	Sheep

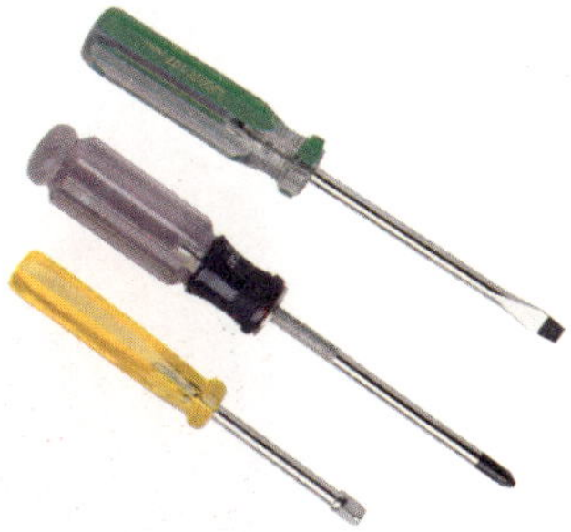

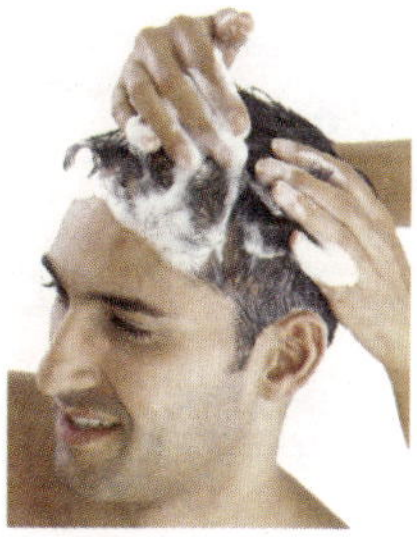

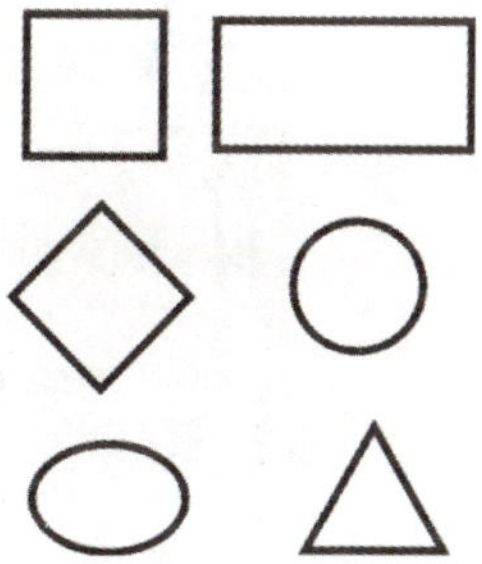

Shell

Shoulder

Sink

Ship

Shovel

Sister

Shirt

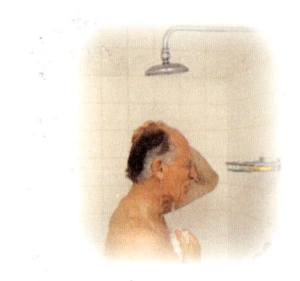
Shower

Skin

Shoe

Shrimp

Skirt

Shorts

Sing

Sky

Sleep

Smile

Soap

Slice

Smoke

Socks

Slide

Snail

Soldier

Slipper

Snake

Son

Smell

Snow

Soup

Space

Spoon

Squirrel

Sparrow

Spray

Stadium

Spectacles

Square

Stain

Spider

Squeeze

Stairs

Spinach

Squid

Stalk

Stamp

Stomach

Straw

Starfish

Stone

Strawberry

Star

Stork

Stream

Steel

Storm

Street

Stick

Stove

Strong

Student

Sunset

Sweater

Sugar

Supermarket

Sweet

Sun

Sushi

Swim

Sunflower

Swallow

Sword

Sunrise

Swan

Syrup

T t

Tag

Tart

T-shirt

Tail

Tattoo

Table

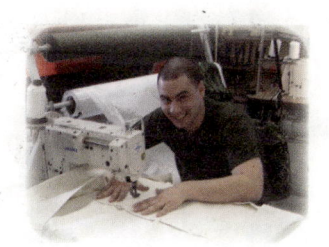

Tailor

Taxi

Tablet

Tank

Tea

Tadpole

Tap

Teacher

Team

Telescope

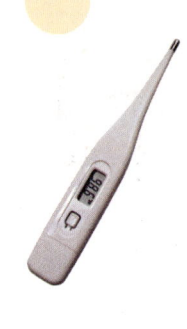
Thermometer

Tear

Temple

Thief

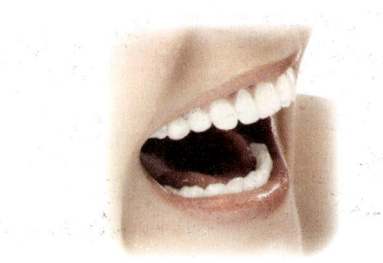
Teeth

Tennis

Thorn

Telephone

Tent

Thread

Telephone booth

Termite

Throat

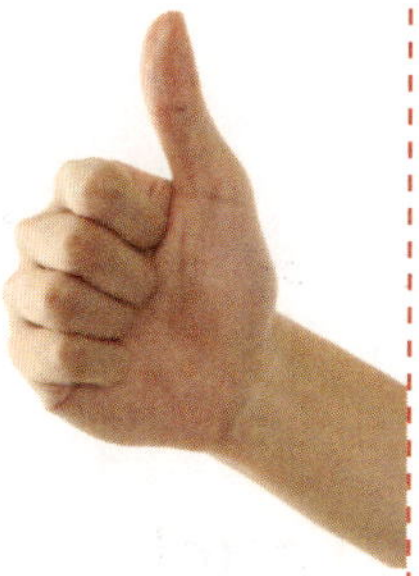

Thumb	Time	Toaster
Thunder	Tin	Toe
Ticket	Tiptoe	Toffee
Tie	Toad	Tomato
Tiger	Toast	Tomb

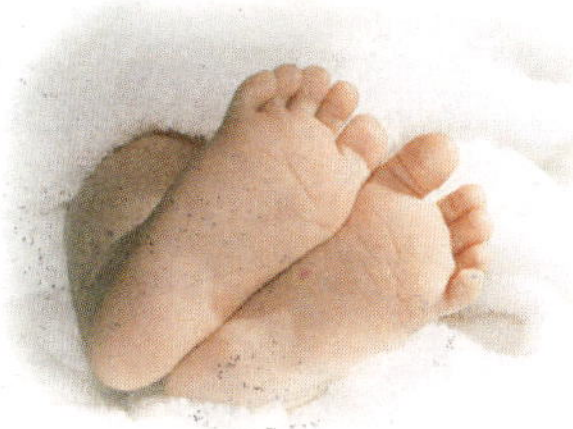

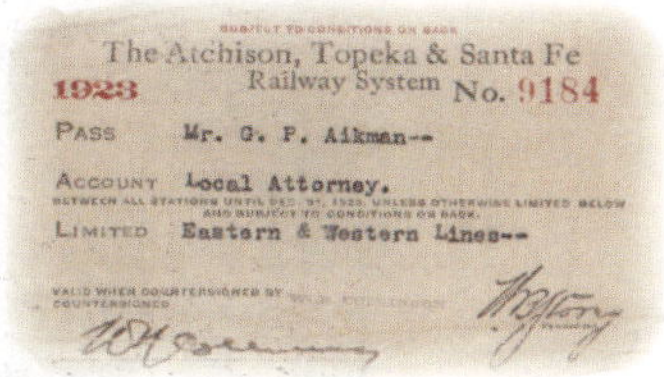

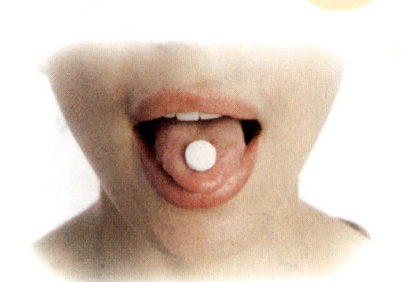
Tongue

Torch

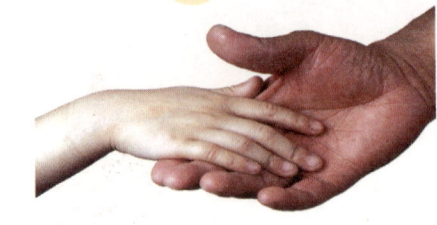
Touch

Tonic

Tortilla

Towel

Tool

Tortoise

Tower

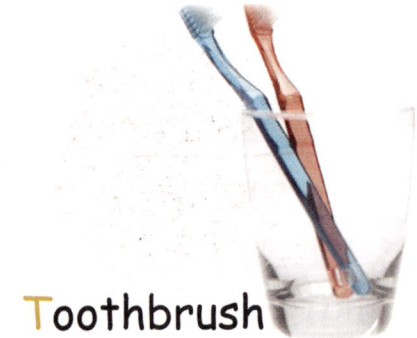
Toothbrush

Toss

Town

Toothpaste

Toucan

Toy

Track

Tram

Treasure

Tractor

Trampoline

Tree

Traffic

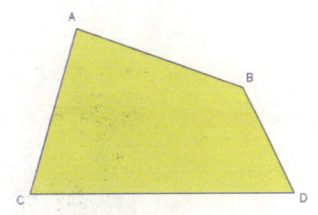

Trapezium

Triangle

Traffic light

Trash can

Tricycle

Train

Treadmill

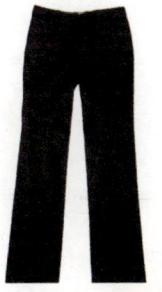

Trouser

Truck

Tumbler

Turkey

Trumpet

Tuna

Turkey vulture

Trunk

Tunnel

Turnip

Tube

Turban

Twig

Tulip

Turbine

Typewriter

Uu

Unicycle

Upstairs

Umbrella

Uniform

Urn

Uncle

Up

Utensil

Vv

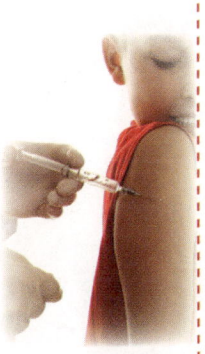
Vaccine

Vacation

Vacuum cleaner

Vegetable

Valley

Vest

Visitor

Van

Village

Vapour

Violet

Vulture

Vase

Violin

Volcano

Ww

Wall

Wash

Wafer

Walrus

Washerwoman

Wake

Wand

Washing machine

Walk

Wardrobe

Wasp

Walker

Warm

Waste

Watch

Watermelon

Weather

Watchman

Wave

Web

Water

Weak

Weed

Watering can

Weapon

Weevil

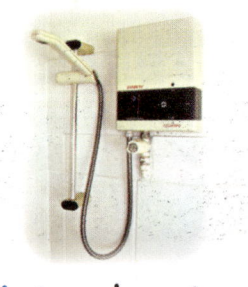
Water heater

Wear

Weep

Weight

Whisper

Wind

Well

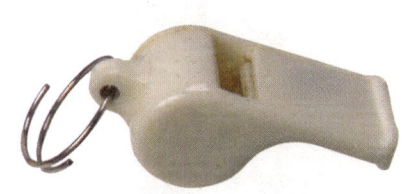
Whistle

Windmill

Wet

White

Window

Whale

Wife

Wing

Wheel chair

Win

Wipe

Wiper

Wood

Worm

Woodpecker

Wrap

Wire

Wool

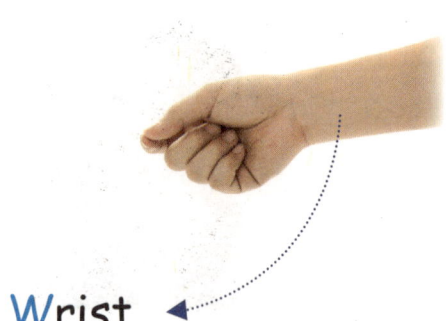

Wrist

Witch

Worker

Write

Wolf

World

Wrong

Xerox

Xbox

X-ray

Xylophone

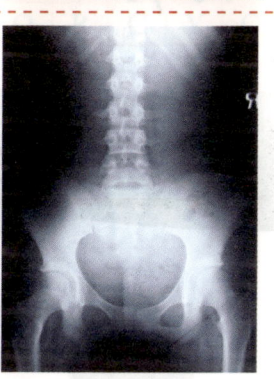

Yak

Yawn

Yacht

Yard

Year

Find and circle the words given below in the word search box.
Remember that the words can be hidden in any direction. Have fun.

T	P	A	R	A	C	H	U	A	F	V	E	D	M
R	S	O	H	E	Z	T	N	N	M	X	L	U	I
A	P	S	D	W	S	A	X	A	W	J	I	K	N
M	E	T	P	F	N	T	O	B	T	R	E	L	J
P	C	R	L	A	Z	V	A	Z	A	S	C	F	E
O	T	I	B	M	R	X	U	U	E	M	L	U	C
L	A	D	A	T	M	A	Q	L	R	F	V	R	T
I	Q	A	N	W	J	A	C	V	M	A	A	N	I
N	U	R	A	T	U	A	K	H	X	V	N	I	O
E	A	K	N	F	T	J	L	J	U	W	D	T	N
R	E	L	E	C	T	R	I	C	I	T	Y	U	T
B	E	L	E	L	S	F	W	D	T	L	E	R	O
Q	R	P	T	O	R	N	A	M	E	N	T	E	K
K	S	R	K	P	A	R	R	O	T	Y	B	U	S

PARACHUTE

RESTAURANT

SPECTACLES

TRAMPOLINE

ORNAMENT

BANANA

FURNITURE

AQUARIUM

ELECTRICITY

INJECTION

Do you like eating fruits and vegetables? Look at the pictures given below and solve the crossword.

ACROSS

1.
2.
3.
4.
5.
6.

DOWN

7.
8.
9.
10.
11.
12.